Law Of Attraction

All That Pertains To The Theory Of The Law Of Attraction

Introduction

I want to thank you and congratulate you for downloading the book, *"Law Of Attraction - All That Pertains To The Theory Of The Law Of Attraction."*

The law of attraction is something almost everyone has experienced, on a conscious or subconscious level at one time or the other. Even as we speak, you have experienced the law of attraction at some point in your life.

Do you doubt this immutable fact? Consider this:

Look back to all those times when you were thinking about someone, your phone started ringing with the person you were thinking of on the other end of the line, or the time when you were thinking about someone, and out of nowhere, you bump into the person on the street.

You may choose to label these things mere 'coincidences,' 'luck,' or 'fate' because a part of you finds it difficult to accept the existence of energy in sync with your thoughts, an energy capable of attracting the things you want.

This energy is the universal energy. You can tap into this energy to transform every aspect of your life and attract everything you desire. How do you do that; how do you tap into this power? Well, you use the law of attraction. What is the law of attraction?

This book will teach you everything about the law of attraction, how it works, and then detail how you can consciously begin to use it to get the things you want whether these things are the ideal relationship, a good job, better health, money, you name it.

Thanks again for downloading this book, I hope you enjoy it!

Table of Contents

The Law Of Attraction Explained

To understand the law of attraction as best as anyone can hope to, we need to dissect it and look at various things such as:

Definition Of The Law Of Attraction

There are really no solids; every object in the universe is a constituent of several atoms, molecules, and cells (in the case of humans) bonded together. This means as humans, we are simply a mass of energy rich bonded cells and molecules. The energy in us can connect with the energy outside us just as magnets can connect with each other and electricity can pass through anything that acts as a conduit.

Now, when you conceive thoughts in your mind or you speak specific words out of your mouth, it connects the external energy around you and then begins to connect with other energies that then attract circumstances, people, and opportunities that can bring you the thing you desire.

The law of attraction is not magic: *you do not just sit somewhere and think about driving a luxury car and then bam! It appears at your doorstep.* No, that is not how the law of attraction works. The law works as follows: you think about driving a luxury car, you continue positively focusing on driving this luxury car so you can attract positive energy to your thoughts. The law of attraction sets out to work, it begins to attract business opportunities, or other opportunities that help you make money so you can afford the luxury car or anything else you desire.

The law of attraction requires you to have some level of faith: *you have to trust the universe to bring you the things you desire.* The moment you begin to doubt the effectiveness of the law of attraction, you will have released negative energy, and because of such negative thinking, you may be unable to attract what you want.

The History

The law of attraction is not in any way new. It is not something that started this century or the last: it has been in existence long before man became conscious of it.
Religious teachers like Jesus Christ and the Buddha spoke repeatedly about attracting things through positive thinking. Both spiritual leaders (Jesus and Buddha) spoke strongly against harboring a negative mindset and strongly encouraged positive thinking even though they did not exactly label it "The law of attraction."
For instance, in one of his teachings, the Buddha said, *"All that we are is as a result of what we have thought."*
In modern times, authors like Wallace Delois Wattles, Helena Petrovna Blavatsky, Charles Francis Haanel, and very recently, Rhonda Byrne who wrote the bestselling book 'The Secret," have all made the law of attraction popular.

Celebrities And The Law Of Attraction

Another thing that has made the law of attraction even more popular is the various testimonies from different public figures and celebrities who openly say they have used the law of attraction to attract the fame and wealth they enjoy today.

Arnold Schwarzenegger, for instance, never hesitates to tell the whole world how the law of attraction helped him win various beauty pageants and become a governor in California. Oprah Winfrey dedicated a segment of her talk show to talking about the law of attraction and how it helped her land a major movie role and how she has been using it to attract different things into her life.

Will Smith and Jim Carrey are also amongst some of the famous celebrities who give credit to the law of attraction for the success and fame they currently enjoy. Jim Carrey's story is a particularly interesting one. Jim Carrey wrote himself a check of $10 million he wanted to earn from acting and attached a timeframe to it. He carried this self-written check around and guess what? Before the time had elapsed, Jim was earning as much as double that amount.

We might have looked at people who claim that the law of attraction worked for them but is there scientific evidence to show that the law of attraction actually works? Let us learn more about this in the following chapter.

Does The Law Of Attraction Work?

It is important to understand that each of us sends out into the universe, positive or negative vibrations. These vibrations are what we have come to know as vibes. For instance, if you feel good around a particular person or place, you may say that you get *"good vibes"* from the person or if the opposite is the case, you may say you get *"bad or 'negative vibes."* This means your moods and feelings emit vibrations that are either positive or negative.

Now, the law of attraction responds to the vibrations you emit. It matches your vibrations; positive for positive and negative for negative.

Have you ever woken up on a certain morning feeling irritated, bad, and cranky only for the whole day to end up being a complete mess (nothing worked out as planned and you were barely happy). That is the law of attraction works. The moment you woke up feeling bad, you unconsciously sent out some negative vibrations and the law of attraction responded by matching these vibes with negative energy, which is why negative occurrences continued to happen around you throughout the day.

Sometimes, when the same thing repeatedly happens to you, you become sad and dejected; you may even start believing you have bad luck, which is why the same thing keeps happening to you. Have you ever considered the fact that you might have been unconsciously sending out negative vibrations concerning that aspect of your life and as a result, negative things continue to happen to you?

The law of attraction begins the moment you observe a situation in your life. For instance, upon observing your past or current relationships, your financial situation, job, and so on. The moment you begin observing, you send out a vibration that could be positive or negative.

When you think about your past relationships, if what comes to your mind is how these relationships were hurtful and how your past relationships never end well, you send out a negative vibration. As soon as you emit a negative vibration, the law of attraction matches it with negative energy. The negative energy begins to operate and negative things begin to happen so that at the end of the day, you get just what you had pictured or imagined.

You may probably be thinking that this whole thing sounds like a plot of a science fiction script, and you may be wondering if there is any scientific evidence for this.

Well, there is.

Mirror Neurons

Mirror neurons were initially noticed in monkeys and later in humans. Mirror neurons are responsible for humans behaving in the same pattern or mimicking someone after they have observed them for some time. For instance, if you spend a lot of time with someone, you will start picking up some of the person's manners and habits. Mirror neurons are present in the parietal and pre-motor cortex of the brain, the areas responsible for movement and attention in the body.

Mirror neurons show there is a connection between people's brain, a kind of energy that can fire up another person's brain to cause them to act in a similar way. This also means the brain can communicate with external forces (energy).

Physician Robert Lanza once wrote, *"We are all the ephemeral forms of a consciousness greater than ourselves. The mind of every human being is instantaneously connected to each other as a part of every mind existing in space and time. Quantum mechanics tells us that all human minds are united in one mind and the entities of the universe – electrons, photons, galaxies, and the like – are floating in a field of mind that cannot be limited within a restricted space or period."*

Intention and Action

Another scientific justification for the law of attraction lies with the fact that the portion of the brain responsible for intention lies very close to the portion responsible for action. For action to occur, intention needs to be strong enough. Before you can lift your hands, you must think about it, thereby creating intention, and then your brain communicates with the portion responsible for action and then before you know it, your hands are up.

Because it happens so fast, you barely notice all the processes and communications that had to take place within your body before you could carry out that simple enough action of raising up your hands.

So, what does this have to do with the law of attraction?

When you focus your attention on a particular action for long enough, whether that action is positive or negative, those things will most likely begin to occur. Not just because your attention and action will remain directed towards that thing you want, but also because the energy created by your thoughts is strong enough to attract external energy that match the ones you have created so that things will begin to occur just how you have imagined, wished, or desired.

The Law Of Attraction And Negative Thinking

It is okay to be skeptical about the law of attraction and its ability to work especially if you have not tried it and confirmed it works. In truth, this thing sounds excessively easy: how can *you just continuously focus your thoughts on something and you get it*, does that not sound like Santa Claus for adults.

However, the truth is that no matter how skeptical you are about the law of attraction, it works. When I first heard about it, I thought it sounded dumb too but it was not long before I got my opportunity to try it out.

I needed a ticket to travel to see a very important client who was going to give me a contract worth good money, money that could change my life. I was very low on cash and did not even know how I was going to afford the ticket but I started packing my luggage for the trip and making travel arrangements.

I had my luggage packed and set to go but no ticket. I even got a small novel to read on the trip. I did not know how, but I knew I was going on that trip and continued to visualize myself closing the deal.

I was shocked to my bone marrow when another client called that afternoon to say that they were going to clear their outstanding debt for a job I had completed that afternoon. The payment came as a surprise because it usually took that client a few weeks to pay his bills but for whatever reason, the client decided to make an early payment and thanks to that, I had more than enough money to pay for my ticket, go on my business trip, and take an extra holiday if I so wished.

That was how I became 'initiated' into the 'club.'

There is no doubt, however, that so many people have given up on the law of attraction and would argue that it does not work.

The law of attraction is not partial: *there is no reason why it would work for some and not work for others.* This therefore means that for it not to work there must be something hindering the effectiveness of the law. This thing is negative thinking.

Negative thinking is always a hindrance. Remember we mentioned your thoughts create energies that attract like energies – positive for positive and negative for negative. When you focus on negativity, you attract negativity and bad experiences. Negative thinking also reprograms your brain to adapt to negativity and that way, you only attract an abundance of negative things.

Before you start using the law of attraction, you have to deal with negative thinking. Address your emotions concerning the things you want to attract, and try to eliminate all negative thoughts around it. Always approach the law of attraction with a clear and positive mind free from any form of doubt or negativity.

For the law of attraction to work, you also need to have a specific result in mind. Be clear about what you want: *do not just think about having any job, be specific about the kind of job you want, the role or position you would occupy, and how much money you would like to earn from that job.* The law of attraction is more effective when you are as specific as can be.

Lastly, commit to an action plan. Do not just think about having a job without paying attention to the effort you will need to put to get that job. As stated earlier, the law of attraction is not magic, and as you continue focusing on creating positive energies to attract that job, you have to take any necessary actions that will help you land the job. For instance, you can send out applications, scouting for vacancies, and so on.

How To Use The Law Of Attraction

There exists different law of attraction techniques you can use to attract the things you desire. These techniques are effective ways to attract anything you want whether love, wealth, success, or material possessions. Let us get started with the first technique:

Affirmations

Affirmations are short, positive statements about yourself or your situation. Usually your subconscious mind cannot distinguish between true and false; hence, when you say positive statements even when they are not true but are what you want to achieve, your subconscious mind works to make it true. Since the affirmations are positive statements, they work to attract positive things and opportunities in your life. Examples of positive affirmations include:
"I am buying that car in December."
"I have what it takes to manifest my dreams."
"I have the power to attract into my life whatever I desire."
When you continue to make such positive statements, they help you focus on your desires and help you eliminate any doubts or fears that may create negative energies that may prevent you from getting the things you desire.
To use this technique correctly, create your own set of positive affirmations depending on the particular thing you want to attract.
First, you have to be clear on what you want – a new relationship, marriage, money, job, weight loss?

Then begin to create short, positive statements out of the things you want. For instance, if you want to get married, you could create an affirmation stating, "I'm going to be married by June next year." Then think of some of the strengths, advantages, and positive attributes you have that will help you achieve that goal. For instance, you could add, "I'm getting married by this time next year because I have what it takes to attract the right man or woman into my life."

As you create your affirmation, ensure they are positive; thus do not use any negative words like

"I would like to stop drinking",
"I would stop procrastinating"
"I will not gain weight"

Continue using these positive affirmations a few times every day until you get what you want. Do not forget to be specific and attach a timeframe to it too.

Meditation

Most people know meditation as a relaxation exercise; coincidentally, meditation is also one of the techniques you can use to attract the things you desire. Meditation helps you relax and clear your mind so you can focus better on things that matter: the things you want to attract.

Your mind is typically busy every time you are awake and as is often the case, you have dozens of thoughts running through your mind. Meditation helps blank out these other thoughts so you can focus on the thing you want to attract and send out strong, uninterrupted energy to attract your desires.

How To Practice Meditation For Law Of Attraction Purposes

To practice law of attraction meditation, you should:

1. Find a place where you can sit or lie comfortably for 15-30 minutes.

2. Start by freeing your mind of all distracting thoughts and worries. Forget about how crazy your day was/has been and let these 15-30 minutes be all about concentrating on what you wish to attract.

3. Sit or lie quietly as you relax.

4. Focus on your breath and start counting your breaths as you inhale and exhale. This will help you relax.

5. When you feel well relaxed, start imagining being in possession of whatever you desire. If your desire is a marriage for instance, create a mental picture of having a spouse and a happy, satisfied life. Think of all the beautiful things you and your spouse would do together, as well as how happy your life together would be.

Add some excitement to this to create enough positive energy to attract what you desire. You should also continue meditating until you finally get what you desire. This technique will also improve your mental health, focus, and clarity i.e. if you make it a part of your daily life.

Visualization

Have you ever daydreamed? If you have, visualization is a closely related form of this. Visualization is a powerful law of attraction technique where you use your creative imagination and the energy from your thoughts to create your reality. Visualization is my favorite law of attraction techniques because it never disappoints.

Visualization is a simple process almost similar to law of attraction meditation. Here is how to practice it:

1. Choose a comfortable and quiet place.

2. Decide on what you would like to attract.

3. Now, close your eyes and begin visualizing already having that which you desire to attract. If you are trying to attract a new job for instance, you can visualize yourself sitting in your new office or completing your duties at your new job.

4. Now, and this is where visualization slightly differs from regular meditation we already discussed above because when using the visualization technique, you have to involve all your five senses such as sight, touch, taste, smell, and hearing.

As you visualize yourself sitting in that office in your new job, visualize the sound in your office, voices of your colleagues talking or of yourself talking to a client, sounds of work tools and equipment, or any other sound you can attach to the new job. You also need to involve your sense of smell and imagine what the place would smell like.

Involving all your senses makes the visualization stronger and builds a strong positive energy. The more vivid your visualization is, the better your chances of getting what you want.

Self-Hypnosis

Another technique you can use to attract anything you want is self-hypnosis or hypnotherapy. Hypnosis/hypnotherapy helps you break away from distractions and worries about the things you do not want so you can focus on the things you desire.

Naturally, the human mind has a dance-like preoccupation with thoughts, thoughts about undesirable things specifically how to prevent things from going wrong. Self-hypnosis helps break this thought pattern so you can focus on attracting the things you want rather than constantly worrying about the things you do not want.

To practice Hypnotherapy, it is best to seek the assistance of a trained professional who guides you through the process and helps you get into a state of hypnosis. Self-hypnosis on the other hand is a personal experience you can do yourself by helping yourself get into a state of hypnosis.

Here are the steps involved:

1. Decide the exact thing you want to attract. It helps to focus on attracting one thing at a time.

2. Choose a calm and quiet place free from distractions and sit in a chair with your barefoot placed firmly on the floor.

3. Light a candle or place any other object on a table in front of you. The object should be at your eye level. If you do not want to go through too much stress, you can just pick any object that is at your eye level.

4. Start thinking of all the negative or limiting thoughts you would like to get rid of. As you think of them, focus on the object placed in front of you at your eye level.

5. Continue pondering on these limiting thoughts. Your mind may wander during the process; when it does, subtly nudge it back to your object of focus.

6. If you continuously focus on the object at your eye level, you will feel your eyes beginning to close naturally after sometime.

7. At this point, you should feel relaxed and less agitated about those limiting thoughts. Now start slowly directing your attention to whatever you would like to attract.

8. Tell your subconscious you can see yourself having the thing/s you desire and begin to create a vivid picture of having and enjoying those things already just as you did when using the visualization technique.

9. That deep, sleepy state is what we call hypnosis. After visualizing at this stage for a few minutes, you can decide to end your session and bring yourself back to a state of full consciousness.

Self-hypnosis is pretty simple and easy to do; however, if you find it hard to do it, you can consult a professional who can guide you through the first few sessions until you can do it yourself.

Neuro-Linguistic Programming (NLP)

We previously mentioned how the human being is like a walking magnet because of the energies that can interact with external energies. According to the law of attraction, two major actions can create energy; these are thoughts and actions.

Neuro-linguistic programming involves modifying these two important factors and using them positively to attract what you want.

Instead of just visualizing and using your imagination to attract your desires, NLP involves speaking aloud about the things you want so you can attract them. The more you speak about them, the more you believe it and the more this imprints on your mind. Because of the constant build-up of positive energy, your desire becomes stronger and your chances of attracting it become better.

How To Practice NLP For LOA Purposes

To practice Neuro-Linguistic programming, here are the steps you need to take:

1. Decide what you want to attract.
2. Choose a quiet, distraction free place where you can spend at least 15 minutes without interruptions.
3. Create affirmations from those things. For instance, "I will to earn $25, 000 this month"
4. Repeat your affirmations as many times as possible.
5. Visualize already having those things.

6. Start saying your affirmations aloud and this time, try as much as possible to believe you already have what you desire as stated in your affirmation. Strongly believe that these actions can manifest your dreams.

You can use any of these techniques to attract your desires at any time or you can even use multiple techniques to attract one thing. As long as you are consistent and you remove any negative or limiting thoughts, any of these strategies will always work for you no matter what you would like to attract.

When The Law Of Attraction Appears Not To Work

It is common for a few people to achieve no results upon using the law of attraction – you create your intentions, visualize, use all the law of attraction techniques detailed in this book, and yet, nothing happens.

This happens because of what we call resistance. Resistance is an unconscious failure to maintain the same vibrations with your intentions. Resistance happens when you have some fear or doubts about your intentions and sometimes, you may not even realize that you are building resistance. These things just sit there in the background and work against the manifestation of your desires.

When this happens, you may say, "The law of attraction does not work." It is not the law of attraction that does not work; you are the one who is not working it correctly: you have subconsciously created two different intentions.

The first intention is of what you want while the other intention is of what you are afraid of. Because of the two, fear is the stronger emotion, and would thus produce the strongest energy, which is preventing you from attracting what you desire.

How To Overcome Resistance

Before you go on to label the law of attraction as ineffective at helping you manifest your desire, first learn how to overcome resistance. Here are the five steps that will help you overcome resistance.

Step 1: Identify Resistance

The problem is that when we create intentions for the things we want, we completely fail to recognize the side effects of our desires and only focus on the positive and good things we would enjoy when we finally get our desires. Do not take this to mean you should be negative about your desires; however, understand there is a difference between recognizing the consequences of your desires and having fears and doubts about it.

When you ignore the consequences of your desires, your subconscious mind registers I, which creates resistance.

For instance, if your desire is to buy a new car, one of the consequences of owing a car is spending money on gas and maintenance. This means that your expenses would typically increase. If you are currently struggling with your finances, buying a car means extra financial challenges.

You however decide to ignore this because you remain focused on the beautiful idea of owning a car. This, however, does not escape your subconscious mind; your subconscious registers this and creates resistance that keeps you from achieving your desires.

To prevent resistance, identify the consequences of your desires before you start using the law of attraction. Identify these consequences without judgment and figure out how you shall tackle these side effects or consequences so you can avoid subconscious resistance.

Step 2: Monitor Your Moods

The next step towards overcoming resistance is constantly noticing your mood so you can catch yourself whenever fear or doubts crop up or immediately notice resistance building up.

Even though resistance registers on your subconscious, you can still notice it if you pay close attention.

Step 3: Convert Your Resistance to Affirmations

When you have identified resisting thoughts, create positive affirmations out of them so you can use them to create positive energy and attract your desires.

For instance, you can create an affirmation like "Yes, a new car shall increase my expenses, but it will also help me save money on commuting to work as well as the time wasted on the commute to work."

This is a very effective way to eliminate resistance especially if you continue to repeat these affirmations until you finally get what you want to attract.

Step 4: Increase Your Vibrational Energy

When your vibrational energy is not strong enough, it creates resistance. When you are not happy, anxious, stressed, or tense, this state reduces your vibrational energy. You should therefore try to remain in a good and relaxed mood. Engage in activities you love and be around people who make you happy. This will speed up the process of attracting the things you desire.

Step 5: Practice Gratitude

Best-selling author, philanthropist, and public speaker Sarah Ban Breathnach says, *"Gratitude is the most passionate transformative force in the cosmos. If you give thanks for five gifts every day, in two months, you may not look at your life in the same way as you might now."*

Unknown to many, gratitude and the law of attraction work hand in hand. Gratitude means you recognize the efforts the universe played in bringing you your desires and by acknowledging this, you are sharpening your vibrational energy and creating harmonious coexistence with the energy in the universe.

A lack of gratitude for what you already have may prevent you from receiving more especially when you are using the law of attraction to manifest your desire.

The law of attraction does not work well with whining and complaining: you have to learn how to be grateful for what you already have because only then will you attract more and achieve more.

Every day before you use any of the law of attraction techniques, think of at least 21 things you are grateful for and say your gratitude aloud. You should also practice gratitude towards the things you have not received and the things you want to attract because being grateful now for the things you want to manifest confirms to the universe that what you want is yours for the taking and that you are open to receiving it. It energizes the law of attraction, enabling you to manifest quickly.

Conclusion

Thank you again for downloading this book!
As you may have learned, personal problems are nothing if not self-creations. Whatever you have now – negative or positive – you have attracted through thoughts, words, and attitudes.
Now that you know this, you can begin using the law of attraction properly; rather than use it to attract negativity through focusing on fear and doubts, you can begin consciously using it to change your life and attract your heart desires.
Do not forget to practice the principle of ask, believe, and receive. For the law of attraction to work, you have to believe in its powers and ability to manifest your heart's desires.

Finally, if you enjoyed this book, would you be kind enough to leave a review for this book on Amazon?

Click here to leave a review for this book on Amazon!

Thank you and good luck!

Check Out My Other Books

Below you'll find some of my other popular books that are popular on Amazon and Kindle as well. Simply click on the links below to check them out. Alternatively, you can visit my author page on Amazon to see other work done by me.

Paleo: Paleo For Beginners Lose Weight And Get Healthy With These 30 Paleo Recipes

Meditation: Meditation For Beginners How To Relieve Stress, Anxiety And Depression, Find Inner Peace And Happiness

Juicing: Juicing For Beginners Secrets To The Health Benefits Of Juicing 30 Unique Recipes

If the links do not work, for whatever reason, you can simply search for these titles on the Amazon website to find them.